YOUTH WITH CONDUCT
DISORDER

In Trouble with
the World

HELPING YOUTH WITH MENTAL, PHYSICAL, AND SOCIAL CHALLENGES

Title List

*YOUTH WITH CONDUCT
DISORDER*

In Trouble with
the World

*by Kenneth McIntosh
and Phyllis Livingston*

Mason Crest Publishers
Philadelphia

Mason Crest Publishers Inc.
370 Reed Road
Broomall, Pennsylvania 19008
(866) MCP-BOOK (toll free)
www.masoncrest.com

First printing

1 2 3 4 5 6 7 8 9 10

ISBN 978-1-4222-0133-6 (series)

Library of Congress Cataloging-in-Publication Data

McIntosh, Kenneth, 1959-

Youth with conduct disorder : in trouble with the world /
by Kenneth McIntosh and Phyllis Livingston.

p. cm. — (Helping youth with mental, physical, and
social challenges)

Includes bibliographical references and index.

ISBN 978-1-4222-0140-4

1. Conduct disorders in children—Juvenile literature. 2.
Conduct disorders in adolescence—Juvenile literature. 3.
Problem youth—Juvenile literature. I. Livingston, Phyllis,
1957- II. Title.

RJ506.C65Y45588 2008

618.92'89—dc22

2007006743

Interior pages produced by
Harding House Publishing Service, Inc.
www.hardinghousepages.com
Interior design by MK Bassett-Harvey.
Cover design by MK Bassett-Harvey.
Cover Illustration by Keith Rosko.
Printed in the Hashemite Kingdom of Jordan.

The creators of this book have made every effort to provide
accurate information, but it should not be used as a substitute for
the help and services of trained professionals.

Contents

Introduction

We are all people first, before anything else. Our shared humanity is more important than the impressions we give to each other by how we look, how we learn, or how we act. Each of us is worthy simply because we are all part of the human race. Though we are all different in many ways, we can celebrate our differences as well as our similarities.

In this book series, you will read about many young people with various special needs that impact their lives in different ways. The disabilities are not *who* the people are, but the disabilities are an important characteristic of each person. When we recognize that we all have differing needs, we can grow toward greater awareness and tolerance of each other. Just as important, we can learn to accept our differences.

Not all young people with a disability are the same as the persons in the stories. But you will learn from these stories how a special need impacts a young person, as well as his or her family and friends. The story will help you understand differences better and appreciate how differences make us all stronger and better.

—*Cindy Croft, M.A.Ed.*

Did you know that as many as 8 percent of teens experience anxiety or depression, and as many as 70 to 90 percent will use substances such as alcohol or illicit drugs at some time? Other young people are living with life-threatening diseases including HIV infection and cancer, as well as chronic psychiatric conditions such as bipolar disease and schizophrenia. Still other teens have the challenge of being "different" from peers because they are intellectually gifted, are from another culture, or have trouble controlling their behavior or socializing with others. All youth with challenges experience additional stresses compared to their typical peers. The good news is that there are many resources and supports available to help these young people, as well as their friends and families.

The stories contained in each book of this series also contain factual information that will enhance your own understanding of the particular condition being presented. If you or someone you know is struggling with a similar condition or experience, this series can give you important information about where and how you can get help. After reading these stories, we hope that you will be more open to the differences you encounter in your peers and more willing to get to know others who are "different."

—*Carolyn Bridgemohan, M.D.*

Chapter 1
Angry Young Man

Sometimes, *Karma guides your destiny, like a great wave rolling irresistibly across the great deep.* Looking back, that's the way Grizz Sanchez remembered the day he first spoke to Dirk Hayden.

It was a lovely, pure-blue-sky day in Huntington Beach, and Grizz had just finished shaping a new single-fin Malibu at his store, Grizzly Surf Shop. He was tired of the smell of foam and fiberglass, but in almost three decades of his trade, Grizz had never been a slave to the working hours posted on his shop window. When the breezes and waves beckoned, the veteran shaper hung an informally scrawled sign on the front door handle: *Gone Surfin'*. As far as he knew, Grizz had never lost a customer doing that; and if he did they were probably barneys anyway. The dudes would come back when Grizz was in the store.

He slipped off a t-shirt and pulled a rash-guard over his bronzed, scarred chest. He was already wearing a tight-fitting pair of board shorts. He gulped down half a bottle of Gatorade and pulled his favorite long board—same one he usually rode for the past decade, dinged all over as it was—off the wall. He headed out the door.

It was a couple of blocks to the beach, and in that short space a half dozen old friends and acquaintances exchanged greetings with him. The barrel-chested, squinty-eyed man with the long grey ponytail was a well-loved citizen of Surf City, a true soul surfer.

He was about to be disappointed, however. Grizz reached the water's edge and stood still for a moment, eyes closed, sensing the wind. He looked out over the water, noting the direction and timing of the swells, casting his gaze past the throng of tourists, families, and Boogie Boarders, noting who was in the water and how they lined up for the break. Then, just as he bent down to fasten the leash on his ankle, he heard a loud whistle and watched blackball flags pop up on the lifeguard stations.

Shoot.

No surfing today at this beach; too many bodies in the water to be safe. He'd have to walk back to the shop, get in his jeep, and drive down the coast till he found an open shore. *Didn't used to be like this in the seventies and eighties,* he mused. Too many tourists in the ocean now.

Still, it was a lovely afternoon, so Grizz decided to sit for a few minutes; after decades of living by the beach, he still enjoyed the people, the sand, the sun, and the ocean— the whole beautiful scene. Other surfers came in with their boards, trudged past him, or set themselves down on the sand: the Gidgets in their Roxy clothes who were now as well respected in the waves as their male counterparts, the new-school boys with their thrusters, and middle-aged guys with their long boards. Children continued to laugh and splash in the foamies at the ocean's edge, teen boys and girls chased and hugged, moms built sand castles with their little ones as waves lapped at scooped-out moats. *Yeah, Grizz thought, Surf City is alright—even if it is over-run most of the time. God made this place so people could soak in the sun, laugh and play in the big wet, just what they're doing now.*

His pleasant thoughts were interrupted by a tinny voice, a lifeguard calling through his megaphone. "The blackball flag is up. Surfers, get out of the water. I repeat—get *out* of the water."

Grizz stood and shaded his eyes, peering out into the waves. There was a young man with long red hair out there, pulling into a tube. He rocketed along the inside, his hand barely visible against the curling lip, then popped out the other end, jumping his board up and down in victory. For an instant, Grizz smiled. *That kid can ride*, he thought, but his smile quickly faded. A little girl in a plastic inflatable vest was right in front of the emerging surfer.

At the last instant the wave rider saw her and threw his weight to the side.

The board jetted past the little girl's head.

Fins tore her inflatable float to shreds.

Idiot, it's stuff like that gives the sport a bad name, Grizz fumed.

"You with the surfboard, get out of the water *now*." The lifeguard was clearly angry.

Grizz expected the red-haired kid to swim in and get a tongue-lashing, but to his amazement, the lone surfer threw an obscene gesture toward the shore, turned, and paddled out again. The lifeguard picked up his walkie-talkie and a minute later, two guards on Jet-Skis came bucking across the waves toward the young man. Still amazingly undaunted, the red-headed boy popped up on another wave and zig-zagged into the shore, pursued by two angry lifeguards on their watercraft. As he did so, he barely missed hitting a woman and her two blond-haired toddlers playing where the wave broke.

The defiant surfer ripped off his leash, then sprinted onto the beach, heading for the parking lot, obviously hoping to avoid an encounter with the authorities—but a white

SUV with siren wailing pulled up in front of him. Two red-suited beach protectors, a man and a woman, stepped out to confront him. Grizz was standing a dozen yards away, but he could hear the boy cussing and see his wild gestures. *Kid doesn't have sense to be embarrassed,* Grizz thought, amazed.

The red-headed youngster shoved his way past the lifeguards, giving one of them a hard push. For a moment, Grizz wondered if there was going to be a fight, but the guards were evidently in no mood to make an arrest and the kid headed up the shore, still shouting. The guards let him go.

The kid's head was turned, and he almost bumped into Grizz. Grizz cleared his throat loudly, and the kid's head jerked forward. Their eyes met. The young man's dark green eyes flashed fire; those bulging eyes, combined with his bright red carrot top, made him appear daunting indeed.

The boy paused for an instant. "Hey, you're Grizz Sanchez, aren't you?"

"And who might you be?"

"Dirk Hayden. I've seen you in your shop."

"Yeah, that looks like one of my boards, but I don't recall sellin' it to ya."

"Oh, yeah. You made this one—and it rocks. You make the best boards in town; everyone knows that. But I couldn't afford a new one; don't have money like the stuck-up folks do. Won it gamblin'."

"Nice to know purchasers take such good care of my products." Grizz smiled. "Looks like one I made more than a decade ago; someone did a good job patching it."

"Yeah, I fixed it up after I scored it."

"Some pretty fancy moves out there today."

"That was nothin'. You woulda seen me shred, but those idiots in the towers felt like ruinin' my fun today."

Grizz scrunched up his tanned forehead. "Ever occur to you that maybe there's a good reason for blackball flags? I was hoping to hit the water myself, but God didn't make that there ocean just for you and me. You pret' near hit a little girl out there."

"Oh, get off it, Pops—I saw her, and I missed her, didn't I?"

"Not by much. What you got against lifeguards, anyway?"

"They're all full of themselves. Like cops."

"They're doin' their job, keepin' things in order." Grizz pulled a cigarette pack out of his gear bag and tapped a clove cig from the wrinkled white container. He changed the subject, "Tell me, you ever enter competitions? You've got excellent form—when you're not runnin' people over."

Dirk's face reddened, his eyes protruded still more, and he clenched his fists. "You're dissin' me, arncha, hodad?"

"Don't get all heated. Just asked you a question."

The younger man relaxed a bit. "Yeah, I've been in competitions. And I would have won last year's open—I was the best dude in the lineup—'cept that stupid judge from Hawaii got all mad about something I said and kicked me out of the event."

"Well, now that you mention it," Grizz paused for a moment, recalling, "I do know you. You were all riled up because you thought that Aussie kid cut in on you. You threatened to beat that judge up."

"Yeah. I was right, too—those jerks on the judges' panel don't ever see when stuff like that happens."

"Sounds like that hurt. What did your folks have to say about it?"

Dirk shrugged. "I ran away from home two years ago. Mom left my old man and me a couple of years before that, saying something about 'I can't control that kid anymore.' My old man's a jerk. I couldn't stand living with him so I left him. I just hang out or crash in people's houses."

"You in school?"

"What is this, an interrogation?"

"Just askin'. I like to know the young guys and gals out on my boards—and you look to me like someone with a future in surfing."

"Get real. I dropped out of high school, since you ask. Shore View sucks."

Grizz shook his head. "Son, looks to me like you're carrying a chip on your shoulder the size of Catalina Island."

"Buzz off."

Dirk picked up his board, glared, and started past the older man. Grizz lit up a cigarette and absently sucked on the cancer stick. He called after the young man, "Wanna' work in my shop?"

"Huh?"

"I'm offering you a job."

"Now why would you do that?"

"You've got no home, no schooling, and I assume no job. I figured you could use some money, and I like to hire young folks that can surf."

"Get out."

"Nope. For real. Want to work for me?"

"Go jump. You thinkin' you can rehab me?"

"Just offering a job. You want it?"

"No way. I keep my own hours, do whatever I want. Surf all day, get high and pick up chicks at night. When I see somethin' I want, I take it. No one messes with me. Why should I work?"

Grizz shrugged. "Just an idea."

Dirk shook his head and started away, then paused, and finally turned back again. "Hey, Grizz, I'm sorry, dude. You don't want me. Wouldn't do either of us any good. I'm a freak, I tick everyone off. My folks, the other kids, the life-guards, the cops—they all hate me. You would too."

Grizz watched Dirk's back as he walked away. He had a feeling he'd be seeing more of this angry young man.

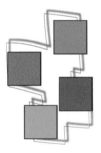

What Is Conduct Disorder?

Teenagers with conduct disorder have repetitive and persistent patterns of behavior in which they violate the rights of others, or violate **norms** or rules that are appropriate for their age. We're not talking here about ordinary adolescent mischief and pranks. Kids with conduct disorders have severe difficulties at home, in school, and in the community; they frequently become sexually active early. Their self-esteem is usually low, although they may project an image of "toughness." Teenagers with this disorder are often described as "bad," "delinquent," or "antisocial," when in reality they have a psychiatric disorder. Some teenagers with conduct disorder may also have symptoms of other psychiatric disorders.

Many factors may contribute to a child developing conduct disorder, including brain damage, child abuse, genetic vulnerability, school failure, and other traumatic life experiences.

Children or adolescents with conduct disorder may exhibit some of the following behaviors:

1. aggression to people and animals

- bullies, threatens, or intimidates others
- often initiates physical fights
- has used a weapon that could cause serious physical harm to others (for example, a bat, brick, broken bottle, knife, or gun)
- steals from a victim while confronting them (in other words, assault)
- engages in physical cruelty against people or animals
- forces someone into sexual activity

Despite actually having low self-esteem, a teenager with conduct disorder may present an image of toughness to the world.

Children with conduct disorder are often involved in physical fights, usually initiated by themselves.

2. destruction of property

- deliberately engages in fire setting with the intention to cause damage

- deliberately destroys other's property

3. deceitfulness, lying, or stealing

- has broken into someone else's building, house, or car

- lies to obtain goods, or favors or to avoid obligations

- steals items without confronting a victim (in other words, shoplifting but not breaking and entering)

An individual with conduct disorder often exhibits deceitful behavior such as shoplifting.

Many children with conduct disorder skip school, stay out late at night, or run away from home.

4. serious violations of rules

- often stays out late at night despite parental objections
- runs away from home
- often truant from school

Children who exhibit some of these behaviors should receive a comprehensive evaluation by a skilled professional. Many children with a conduct disorder may have coexisting conditions such as mood disorders, anxiety, **post-traumatic stress disorder**, substance abuse, **ADHD**, learning problems, or thought disorders that can also be treated.

Research shows that youngsters with conduct disorders are likely to have ongoing problems if they and their families do not receive early and comprehensive treatment. Without treatment, many youngsters with conduct disorder are unable to adapt to the demands of adulthood and continue to have problems with relationships and holding a job. They often break laws or behave in antisocial ways.

Chapter 2

Grizzly Surf Shop

I t's not easy doing the right thing; the universe has a way of punishing every good deed. That's how Grizz thought when he looked back later on the day Dirk thought twice about his offer.

Grizz stared at a new carbon-fiber board, on loan from a friend. He ran his hands up and down its polished sides, a quizzical look on his face. The flex seemed wrong . . . the rockers looked odd . . . the fins were an unappealing shape.

"Hey Grizz, you're supposed to ride that thing—not stare at it all day."

It was Josh, the Shore View High kid who worked for Grizz on Saturdays.

Grizz enjoyed it when Josh worked at the store; Josh was a hard person to dislike. Tall, blond, and athletic, he was known as the "Boy Wonder" by the other kids at the high school. He was a successful student, and though he tried to conceal it, Grizz knew Josh had a sharp brain. He was also a fine surfer and skateboarder, fearless and with impeccable balance. Josh was good for business, too. He had introduced a whole new generation of teen surfers to the Grizzly line of surfboards.

"So what do you think of it, Grizz? Think you'll start making new-style boards like that?" Ashley, Josh's girlfriend, leaned over the other side of the counter.

Grizz wouldn't normally encourage the girlfriends of employees to hang around the store, but Ashley was different. Like Josh, she was polite and considerate. She was also a fine surfer, and Grizz had learned it was good business to hand Ashley his new experiments, saying 'Here, Gidj, go try this out." Girls were almost half his business now, and Ashley was a fine representative of the market.

A few years ago, Ashley had been dealt a terrible blow when her friend Stacie died. Before that, Ashley and Stacie were inseparable friends, like twin mermaids in the water. They took turns winning first or second prize at the junior girls' surf events throughout their middle school years. Unfortunately, Stacie was plagued by devastating bouts of sadness her freshman year in high school. Then Stacie had drowned; Grizz had never dared discuss it with Ashley, but he wondered if Stacie's depression had gotten the best of her. He couldn't understand how such an amazing athlete would die accidentally on a flat day in the water. Ashley had stayed out of the ocean for almost a year, but her deepening relationship with Josh had brought her back to the surfing life.

Grizz answered Ashley's question: "No. I can't imagine trying to make something like this. It's actually *molded,* can you believe it? Not sculpted –just poured in a form. What kind of art is that?" Grizz shook his head. "There will always be folks who enjoy the fine lines of a hand-shaped long board with a great big skeg hangin' below the bottom. Not just old-timers like me but kids too. These days there's room in the world for all kinds of boards."

"Right on," said Josh. "Someday I wanna make a hardwood board, like those natives in Hawaii that met Admiral Cook's sailors. Now that is *real* old school."

"Sometimes I wonder which of you two is the older one," Ashley joked. "I love these new boards—I'd buy one tomorrow if I could afford it."

Grizz felt good when Josh and Ashley were in the shop. He'd been married three times; and who could say there wouldn't be a fourth Mrs. Grizz Sanchez? But he'd never stayed married long enough to have kids. Sometimes he was thankful; children seemed like an awful lot of bother. Yet today, bantering with the two teens, he realized how much he missed not having kids of his own.

A shadow fell across the room, and the three glanced at the door. A young man in jeans and a hooded sweatshirt stood there; although the sun was at his back, they could make out wisps of red hair and the gleam of green eyes.

"Hey there," Grizz said, sounding relaxed and jovial. "Dirk, are you here to buy gear, chat, or take me up on my job offer?"

At that last word, Josh and Ashley both widened their eyes. Grizz ignored their startled looks.

"Got busted again shoplifting—freakin' cops are all over me. Can't get nothin' I need. Kinda stinks not havin' money all the time."

"Yes," Grizz agreed, "it does."

"And . . . it would be cool to learn how to make boards. . ."

"It's a wonderful art; very enjoyable," Grizz affirmed.

"So . . . yeah. I'd like to work for you . . . if you'll still let me."

"You bet." Grizz stepped around the corner and put out his hand. Dirk slowly extended his own, shook. "Be here Monday at eight," Grizz said. "Do you have your license?"

Dirk shook his head.

"Then bring your social security number; we'll have to fill some papers out."

Dirk nodded.

"You're gonna have to follow some rules, if you want to work here. No wacky weed when you're in the shop. What you do on your own time is your own thing, but working here for me, we stay clean, okay?"

"Yeah, I can do that," Dirk replied tonelessly.

"And if items come up mysteriously missing, you'll be out of a job."

"Yeah, yeah . . . I understand. Gotta' keep my nose clean to work here, become the establishment. Sucks, but I can hang. See you Monday."

The red-headed boy shuffled out of the shop.

"What are you doing?" Josh blurted, as soon as the glass door swung shut.

"Hiring a new employee. You can only work weekends, and I need more help."

"But Grizz," Ashley wailed, "you don't know about that kid."

"Hmm . . . let me guess." Grizz scratched his nose. "He's a drop out?"

"That's right," Josh retorted, "His dad kicked him out of the house because he was a jerk."

"And he smokes pot and chases every girl in a swimsuit," Grizz continued.

Both teens nodded. Ashley added, "He's violent, he steals stuff, he's been caught tagging, and he harasses the lifeguards."

"Sounds like he'll make a great worker," Grizz chuckled.

"Grizz, we're not joking," Josh pleaded. "I don't like to put anyone down, and my youth pastor says, 'Everyone needs someone to love them,' but—you're making a big mistake."

"This guy's abused almost everyone he's ever met," Ashley added.

"Turn your back, he'll rip off everything in the shop. Why get hurt?" Josh concluded.

"Alright, you've had your say. It's my shop and I'll hire whoever I want. I told that kid he'd have a job here on Monday. He will." Grizz stood and walked slowly into the back of the store.

Josh and Ashley shook their heads.

Grizz passed the saw horses and foam blanks in his workroom, then walked out the narrow door leading into an alley. There, he leaned against the back of the shop, reached in his pocket, and pulled out a crumpled pack of cigarettes. He took one out, produced a lighter from his shirt pocket, lit, and inhaled deeply, slowly, soothingly. Like many his age, Grizz wished he had never started smoking, but he had done so since he was a kid, and it was awful hard to stop now.

He closed his eyes, took another puff, and let his thoughts drift back three decades. He pictured himself, a wiry teen with long wavy hair—always in trouble. Trouble with his parents, with his teachers, with the cops. He'd hated the world then, thought they were all "square," out to ruin his life somehow. Thankfully, there was the ocean—a whole liquid universe of freedom and peace. There had also been one boy, just a year older, who somehow looked past all the yelling, swearing, and hating, and tried to help him. The kid's friendship had been a lifeline, something to hold onto no matter how bad things got.

Grizz wasn't sure if he had straightened out any over the years. He knew his former wives would all argue that he never did grow up, but at least he'd learned to stop hating the world. Once that had happened, he did okay. He thought about Dirk and smiled.

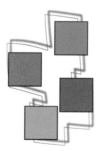

How Does Conduct Disorder Begin?

An adolescent with a conduct disorder often started out with another disorder called oppositional defiant disorder (ODD). A young person with a conduct disorder *behaves* and *acts* in negative way; a child with ODD, however, *talks* in a negative way. Conduct disorder is more serious, but ODD can escalate into conduct disorder.

ODD

All children are oppositional from time to time, particularly when tired, hungry, stressed, or upset. They may argue, talk back, disobey, and defy parents, teachers, and other adults. This is often a normal part of development both for preschoolers between two and three years old and for early adolescents. However, openly uncooperative and hostile behavior becomes a serious concern when it is so frequent and consistent that it stands out as more serious when compared with other children of the same age and developmental level and when it affects the child's social, family, and academic life.

Children with ODD have an ongoing pattern of uncooperative, defiant, and hostile behavior toward authority figures that seriously interferes with their day-to-day functioning. Symptoms of ODD may include:

- frequent temper tantrums
- excessive arguing with adults
- active defiance and refusal to comply with adult requests and rules

Children with oppositional defiant disorder frequently throw temper tantrums.

A child with ODD is easily annoyed by others and she may often show resentment and anger.

- deliberate attempts to annoy or upset people
- blaming others for mistakes or misbehavior
- often being touchy or easily annoyed by others
- frequent anger and resentment
- "mean" and abusive words when upset
- seeking revenge

The symptoms are usually seen in multiple settings—such as on the playground, in the classroom, with friends, and with relatives—but they may be most noticeable at home or at school. Five to 15 percent of all school-age children have ODD.

The causes of ODD are unknown, but many parents report that their child with ODD from an early age was more rigid and demanding than the child's siblings. Biological and environmental factors may have a role.

A child presenting ODD symptoms should have a comprehensive evaluation, since other disorders may be present as well, such as ADHD, learning disabilities, mood disorders (depression, **bipolar disorder**), and anxiety disorders. The symptoms of ODD may not be able to be addressed without treating the coexisting disorder. Some children with ODD may go on to develop conduct disorder.

Treatments for ODD may include:

- parent training programs to help guide the child's behavior
- individual psychotherapy to develop more effective anger management

- family psychotherapy to improve communication
- **cognitive-behavioral therapy** to assist problem solving and decrease negativity
- social skills training to increase flexibility and improve frustration tolerance with peers.

A child with ODD can be very difficult for parents to handle. Parents of these children need support and understanding; they are not "bad" parents. Parents can help their child with ODD in the following ways:

- Always build on the positives; give the child praise and positive reinforcement when he shows flexibility or cooperation.

- Take a time-out or break if you are about to make the conflict with your child worse, not better. This is also good modeling for your child, demonstrating a technique he can also use for handling stress. Support your child if he decides to take a time-out to prevent overreacting.

- Pick your battles. Since the child with ODD has trouble avoiding power struggles, prioritize the things you want your child to do. If you give your child a time-out in his room for misbehavior, don't add on time for arguing. Instead, say something like, "Your time will start when you go to your room."

- Set up reasonable, age-appropriate limits with consequences that can be enforced consistently. Don't take away things that are so far in the future that they are meaningless to the child (such as threatening to cancel their birthday party the following year or cancel an upcoming family vacation).

- Maintain interests other than your child with ODD, so that working with your child doesn't take all your time and energy. Try to work with and obtain support from the other

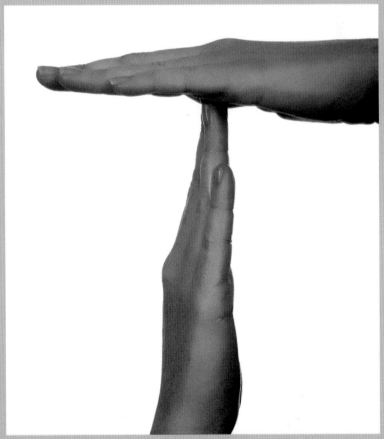

Parents of a child with ODD need to learn new, more effective parenting behaviors. One technique is to take a time-out whenever a conflict seems to be getting worse instead of better.

Parenting a child with ODD can be very stressful. Exercise is a healthy way for a parent to manage her stress.

adults (teachers, coaches, and your spouse or partner) dealing with your child.

• Manage your own stress with exercise and relaxation. Use **respite** care as needed.

Many children with ODD will respond to positive parenting techniques. Parents may ask their pediatrician or family physician to refer them to a child and adolescent psychiatrist, who can diagnose and treat ODD and any coexisting psychiatric condition.

Sometimes, however, for whatever reason, a child with ODD does not get the help he needs. In that case, his condition may escalate into conduct disorder as he gets older and moves toward adolescence. Currently, the research shows that in many respects, conduct disorder is a more severe form of ODD. Severe ODD can lead to CD. Milder ODD usually does not.

Chapter 3

New Kid in the Store

Steady, even rows now, like mowing the lawn."

The electric planer whined as Dirk held it with both hands, a little shaky, guiding the whirling machine along the curved length of a foam board. Both he and Grizz wore paper face masks and old clothes covered with fine white particles from the blank.

"Remember you can always take more off—but you can't ever put it back on. Patience is the key."

Grizz had been teaching people to make surfboards for years, and he took special pleasure in showing this young hot-head the art of shaping. They'd had a few moments of tension, but for the most part Dirk was a surprisingly good employee.

Dirk shut the planer off and wiped foam dust off the blank with a gloved hand, then stepped back to examine his work.

"What do you think?" Grizz asked.

"I went too deep here on the rail. It's not even with the rest of the surface."

"Good eye. You're getting the hang of this."

They were interrupted by a stern voice from the front of the shop. "Is Dirk Hayden back there?"

The elder shaper and his new apprentice exchanged puzzled looks.

"I'm working back here," Dirk replied.

"Huntington Beach Police, we'd like to ask you a few questions."

The red-headed boy tensed and glanced at the rear exit. Grizz shook his head. "Steady. Go talk to the officer."

The two took off their masks and stepped into the front room of the store, foam particles still clinging to their clothes. Two officers stood in front of the counter, one Asian, the other Hispanic, neither smiling.

"You Dirk?"

"Yeah. So?"

"Where were you this morning, between midnight and five AM?"

"Sleeping. What did you think?"

"Don't be smart, boy, just answer the question. Where were you sleeping at?"

"The alley, out back." Dirk nodded toward the rear of the store.

"Was anyone with you? Anyone that can vouch for that?"

Dirk's nostrils flared. "I didn't have any chick with me ... they don't like doing it in the street. And I don't exactly have a big happy family sleeping with me on the pavement. So no, officer, no one can vouch for that. What's this all about, anyway?"

"Don't suppose you've seen this before?" The Latino officer pulled an aerosol can out of a bag. "Or this?" Another can.

"You think I was tagging?"

"You do have an arrest record for it. And you had an altercation last week with the lifeguards, and someone sprayed obscenities all over the guard stations north of the pier."

Grizz could see Dirk was almost jumping out of his skin. He thrust his middle finger up in the air and bit off the two words that went with the hand motion.

"What?"

"You heard me. You jerks have nothing better to do than be hasslin' people all over town."

"Listen, young man." The Asian officer stepped forward, his face just inches from Dirk. "We could haul you in for insulting an officer."

"Yeah? Why doncha? C'mon. Take me. I'll take you both on." Dirk had formed his hands into fists, amped up for a fight.

"Say, Ernie." Grizz spoke calmly, addressing the Latino officer. "How's the wife and niños? Your dad still have that barbershop?"

The Latino officer tapped the Asian on the shoulder, and both of them took a step back. "Hey, Grizz," replied the officer. "Dad's still cutting hair. Kids are fine. Sorry for disturbing things in your shop like this. But this kid here—" He pointed the end of his baton at Dirk, "He's trouble. Got a record a mile long and an inch short of juvey hall. Our expert on graffiti says it's his style, that new taggin' on the guard towers."

"Well," Grizz sighed. "The kid's been in trouble before, for sure, but he's learning a trade from me now. And I don't think he was out taggin' last night because I work him pretty hard at the shop and he probably needed his sleep. But I'm sure, to show you his good feelings toward the law"—he shot a glance at Dirk—"he'd be happy to volunteer to repaint the towers. Not an admission of guilt, mind you, but a way of showing how he cares about our community."

"What the—" Dirk started to shout, but Grizz pinched his shoulder so hard he winced and cut short his exasperated protest.

"You *will* be glad to paint those towers, in exchange for these officers letting you go now, *won't you*, Dirk?" Grizz's voice was firm.

Dirk was still shaking, his fists clenched, face red, almost ready to explode. Somehow, though, he managed to nod.

The Asian officer nodded back to him, both tipped their hats to Grizz, and then they exited the shop.

Dirk turned toward his young protégé. "Better run down to the hardware store and pick up some paint."

"You jerk! Paint those towers? What were you thinking?" Dirk yelled in reply.

"You wanted to go to the police station with them?"

"No, but . . ."

"Think you'd have gotten off any easier? If I'd stayed out of it. If you'd handled it by yourself?"

"No, but . . ."

"But what?"

"It's just taggin'. Not like I hurt somebody."

"So you *did* tag on those towers."

"Yeah. So what? Those freakin' lifeguards deserved it."

"You wanna go through your whole life gettin' in trouble? Want to go to jail? Is that your plan? You should be thankin' me for saving your bacon just now."

Dirk glared at the older man, then spit the words through his teeth: "Thank you."

"You're welcome. " Grizz paused a moment. "Where does that ocean-sized chip on your shoulder come from? Are you really so mad at those cops, or the lifeguards, or is there someone else you're really yelling at when you get so mad like that?"

Dirk stared at the ground, his fists clenched. "You mean my old man?"

"You said that, I'm just askin'."

Dirk shook his head. "I hate him."

"Why?"

"He's a stinkin' hypocrite. He was a marine drill sergeant—all full of patriotic bullcrap and how 'character makes the man' and stuff like that. All my life, he treated me like one of his troops. He ordered me to do everything. Cut me down for the slightest mistake, all the time acting like he was God almighty, totally self-righteous."

"But he wasn't?"

"Ha! Are you kidding? They caught him stealin' government property from his unit—thousands of dollars of electronic stuff and supplies. They gave him a 'dishonorable discharge' but does he ever talk about that? Does he ever admit it? No, he still went around ordering me to do things, telling people about his great career in the military. Liar."

Dirk was trembling, tears glistening in the corners of his eyes. *Well, we've hit a raw nerve here,* Grizz noted silently.

"You know, we look at people as black or white, villains or heroes," Grizz said slowly. "But that's not reality. In fact, we are all shades of grey. We can be real good and real jerks too, sometimes the very same day."

Dirk shrugged, and thrust the back of his hand across his eyes.

"Maybe your dad isn't the monster you see. Maybe he has a good side, too."

"Shut up." Dirk backed away from Grizz. "You think you're a freakin' psychologist?"

Grizz shook his head.

"Everyone's messin' with my head. The whole freakin' world's messin' with me. Leave me alone!" Dirk ran out the front of the shop, leaving a cloud of foam dust in his wake.

Grizz sighed, looked out the big glass windows in front of the store. Bright sun poured in and wispy clouds floated in the sky. He walked behind the counter, pulled out the *Gone Surfin'* sign, and headed for the door.

The next morning, Grizz's sandaled feet scrunched in the sand, still covered with dew from the ocean's spray. He walked over to a lone figure, wrapped in a cheap Mexican blanket, curled in a fetal position asleep on the shore. Grizz nudged him with his toe.

"I see you've got the paint cans ready."

"Huh?"

"Time to wake up, sleepy head. We've got some paintin' to do."

Dirk opened tired eyes, blinked, and sat up slowly.

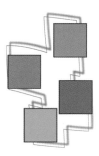

Who Has Conduct Disorder?

Conduct disorder is more common among boys than girls, with studies indicating that the rate among boys in the general population ranges from 6 percent to 16 percent. Meanwhile, the rate among girls ranges from 2 percent to 9 percent. Conduct disorder can have its onset early, before age ten, or in adolescence. Children who display early-onset conduct disorder are at greater risk for longer-lasting difficulties, however, and they are also more likely to have troubled peer relationships and academic problems.

A child who develops conduct disorder before age ten is at greater risk for life-long difficulties.

Abuse is an environmental factor that can trigger conduct disorder.

Among both boys and girls, conduct disorder is one of the disorders most frequently diagnosed in mental health settings. According to the U.S. Department of Health and Human Services, conduct disorders affect 1 to 4 percent of all nine- to seventeen-year-olds, depending on exactly how the disorder is defined. The disorder appears to be more common in cities than in rural areas.

What Causes Conduct Disorder?

Research shows that some cases of conduct disorder begin in early childhood, as ODD, often by the preschool years. In fact, some infants who are especially "fussy" appear to be at risk for developing ODD and conduct disorder. But the precise cause of conduct disorder is not fully known. Studies of twins and adopted children suggest that conduct disorder has both biological (including genetic) and psychosocial components. These social environmental influences include:

- early maternal rejection
- separation from parents, without an adequate alternative caregiver
- early institutionalization
- family neglect
- abuse or violence
- parental mental illness
- parental marital discord
- large family size

- crowding
- poverty

These factors may influence attachment to the parents or to the family unit. Sometimes (but certainly not always) children with one or more of these risk factors may eventually lack regard for the rules and rewards of society.

Physical risk factors that might cause conduct disorder include:

- neurological damage caused by birth complications or low birth weight
- attention-deficit/hyperactivity disorder
- fearlessness and stimulation-seeking behavior
- learning impairments
- autonomic underarousal (a condition where the child needs a higher than normal level of stimulation before she responds)
- insensitivity to physical pain and punishment.

A child with both social deprivation and any of these neurological conditions is most susceptible to conduct disorder.

Since many of the risk factors for conduct disorder emerge in the first years of life, the earlier intervention begins, the more effective it will be. Studies have shown a correlation between the behaviors and attributes of three-year-olds and the aggressive behavior of these children at ages eleven to thirteen. Researchers have developed screening instruments to

Coming from a large family can be a factor in the development of conduct disorder.

Often, a child with conduct disorder benefits simply from having a person care about him.

enable earlier identification of risk factors and signs of conduct disorder in young children.

Training parents of children who are high-risk how to deal with the children's demands may help. Parents may need to be taught to reinforce appropriate behaviors and not harshly punish transgressing ones, and encouraged to find ways to increase the strength of the emotional ties between parent and child. Working with children who are high-risk on social interaction and providing academic help to reduce rates of school failure can help prevent some of the negative educational consequences of conduct disorder.

Sometimes what these young people need most is someone who cares, an emotional and social bond that compensates for the lack of attachments he experienced during his childhood.

Chapter 4

Stormy Day

W-h-h-i-i-r-r. Grizz shut off the planer's drone and set it down on a shelf. He stepped back to look at the board. It wasn't quite what he wanted; seemed like the foam had a defiant mind of its own. *Gotta take a break from this thing,* he thought.

Dirk was up front straightening out the shelves; after last week's tense exchange, the boy had come around nicely. He painted all the lifeguard towers, albeit reluctantly. And he continued to learn the art of shaping; the kid was actually pretty good at it. Grizz stepped out back for a smoke, smiling to himself. Dirk could take care of any customers that came in.

He was surprised by the darkness of the alleyway. Looking up, Grizz saw dark clouds in close formation, coming in low and menacing over the coast. *Rare storm*, he thought, *maybe some great big waves out there*. Unlike the rest of the world, surfers become excited when they see a storm coming: dramatic weather brings big waves. As Grizz lit up a smoke, he thought briefly of heading for the ocean, but then thought again as a bolt of lightning flashed.

Stepping back into the store, he heard voices from the front, Dirk and a female customer. Grizz stepped quietly to the side of the door and stood listening.

"I'm looking for a new rashguard, something that'll stand out in the water."

"Hey, I'd see you in the water whatever you wear."

Grizz grimaced behind the door.

"Is that supposed to be a pick-up line?" The young woman's voice was icy.

"No, no. Just . . . you're a total babe. You'd look great in anything—or nothing."

Grizz groaned quietly.

"I did not come in here to be insulted!"

"I'm not insulting! Come on, you chicks know when you're hot. You like it when guys notice you."

"I've spent years in the water learning the sport— and to Neanderthals like you I'm just a body!"

"That's bad?"

This was going way too far. Grizz swung the door open. Dirk was standing by a clothes rack, smirking, facing a very angry young woman with tanned, muscular arms and legs.

"Hello, Keisha. Nice to see you. Please, forgive anything Dirk here may have said. He's new and—"

"Forgive?" Her voice rose, "*Forgive?* Grizz, you expect me to put up with sexual harassment like this in your store?"

"No, no, that's not what I mean at all—"

"Save your breath. I'm through here. In fact, I'm through with Grizzly Surf Shop—period. I've been thinking I need a newer, more sophisticated board, but I've stuck with you and your old-school products out of respect. I thought you were a cool soul-surfer and all that. But now I know better: you're just a dirty old man letting your muscle boy here hit on the customers. We're through, Grizz. I'm going over to Wavetech, and they'll give me a better sponsorship than you ever could."

The glass door slammed as the girl stormed out.

Grizz hastened out the door after the angered young woman. When he came back, he leaned on the counter and moaned, his head in his hands. "Dirk, did it ever occur to you that women were not made just for your pleasure?"

Dirk scratched his red head. "Not really."

"Do you realize what you just did?"

"Hey, I was having fun—she's just some chick."

"No, Dirk. She is not 'some chick.' She is Keisha Arellano. I don't suppose that name means anything to you?"

"Wait a minute. Keisha . . . the teen women's longboard champion last year?"

"Yes, and the year before that."

"Wow. I didn't know she came here."

Grizz frowned. "She doesn't just 'come here.' We sponsor her. She's our best source of advertisement. Make that, *was* our best source of advertisement. We could see a 20 percent, maybe 30 percent drop in sales . . . because of what *you* just did."

Dirk looked uncomfortable. "Aww, c'mon Grizz. You're joking."

"I wish."

"She'll get over it. Chicks like to put on a show like that."

Grizz shook his head.

"Well, forget her then. Why are we sponsoring girls, anyway?" Dirk headed for the counter but tripped over a display of sunglasses, knocking them to the floor. "Whoops. Sorry."

Grizz sniffed, and his eyes narrowed. "Dirk…Come here."

Dirk stood up. Grizz looked at his eyes. "You're stoned."

"No, I'm not."

"Tell me, with a straight face, you're not on something."

Dirk tried to pull his cheeks taut, then burst into a broad grin. "Hey, Pops, it's just a little weed. Nothing serious."

"I told you, that doesn't come in my store."

Dirk raised his voice. "Don't run my life, old man."

"As long as I pay you, I'm your boss."

"Buzz off."

"That's how the world works, Dirk. There's something called respect. That's how you're supposed to treat your boss and your customers."

Dirk's face turned red. "Don't tell me what to do!"

"I own this shop. I'll tell you what I please."

"Forget your stinking shop!"

Whunk!

Clothing flew from racks.

Wham!

A row of expensive longboards down.

C-r-a-a-sh!

Glass display case: thousand shiny fragments.

Grizz backed away as Dirk shoved past him into the workroom. Grizz shut his eyes and tried to breathe deeply. He heard more swearing and banging from the back room.

Minutes later, the back door slammed shut. Bracing himself, Grizz looked into the work room.

Cans of resin, epoxy, and paints were spilled on the floor and splashed on the walls.

Stacks of precious foam blanks smashed into pieces.

The board Grizz had spent all week meticulously shaping shattered, in pieces on the shop floor.

An earthquake could not have done worse damage.

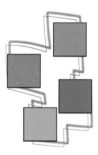

When a young person has a conduct disorder, safety concerns must be addressed. Sometimes it is the personal safety of others in the school, family, or community. Sometimes it is the safety of the possessions of other people in the school, family, or community. Often the safety of the individual himself is a great concern. The people who care about the individual may find it very hard to live with him because they are literally afraid.

What Are the Risks of Conduct Disorder?

Adolescents with conduct disorder may also experience:

- higher rates of depression, suicidal thoughts, suicide attempts, and suicide

Even family members who care about the individual with conduct disorder may find living with him difficult and even scary at times.

Teens with conduct disorder experience high rates of depression and suicidal thoughts.

- academic difficulties
- poor relationships with peers or adults
- sexually transmitted diseases
- difficulty staying in adoptive, foster, or group homes
- higher rates of injuries, school expulsions, and problems with the law

Many people have thought that a conduct disorder is merely the adolescent version of being a criminal. Until recently, young people with conduct disorder were often "written off" as hopeless cases; they were left to the law enforcement community to handle rather than the medical or psychiatric communities.

Behavior problems in school and trouble with grades are common in youth with conduct disorder.

In many cases, a young person with a conduct disorder is also coping with one or more other disorders at the same time. The most common combination is conduct disorder with ADHD; between 30 and 50 percent of all young people with a conduct disorder also have ADHD.

Another common combination is conduct disorder plus depression or anxiety. One-quarter to one-half of children with conduct disorder have either an anxiety disorder or depression. A mood disorder along with conduct disorder often gets missed; adults pay so much attention to the young person's inappropriate behaviors that they may miss the depression or anxiety that accompanies them. Oftentimes, unfortunately,

Until recently a youth with conduct disorder was viewed as hopeless. He would have been left for law enforcement to handle rather than getting treatment.

no one suspects that the young person is depressed until he attempts to commit suicide. Recent studies of teenagers who have committed suicide have found that these individuals are about three times more likely to have a conduct disorder. Suicide is a serious concern when dealing with a young adult who has a conduct disorder.

Conduct disorder plus substance abuse is also very common. Compared with young people who do not have conduct disorders, adolescents who have conduct disorder are three times more likely to smoke cigarettes, 2.5 times more likely to drink, and five times more likely to use marijuana—and they are 5.5 times more likely to be addicted to cigarettes, six times more likely to be alcoholics, and seven times more likely to be addicted to marijuana.

Other common associations with conduct disorders are learning disorders, bipolar disorder, and **Tourette's syndrome**. Very rarely is a diagnosis of "pure conduct disorder" made.

Chapter 5
Ominous Fins

The door's been jimmied—and two hundred dollars are missing from the register." Josh's voice was high-pitched; he was more upset than Grizz had seen him in a long time.

"Wasn't there a real pretty board in the front window, with mother-of-pearl inlays?" Ashley asked. "That's missing, too."

The three had arrived at the shop to open it. Even before stepping inside, they saw obscene words sprayed in bright paint all across the glass front of the store. It was a devastating sight after they had spent two days fixing the mess Dirk left from his rampage in the back room.

"It was Dirk," Ashley declared.

"It's so something he would do," Josh seconded.

Grizz sighed. "I've had this shop for decades—this hasn't happened before. It is funny that it happened now."

"We need to call the police right away." Ashley's voice quavered with emotion. "They should find that idiot and put him in jail where he belongs. He's a menace."

"And then there's this mess," Josh said, and Grizz thought he was fighting to hide a tremble in his voice too. "Where do we start, Grizz?"

Grizz closed his eyes; for a moment, he was mentally elsewhere. Then he opened them, stared at the two teens and the graffiti-covered shop window, glanced toward the place where the most valuable board in the shop had been sitting when he left . . . and smiled. "This would be a good day to take that new carbon board to the water and see how she works."

"Huh?"

"Surf report said nice even waves out there. Ocean should be warm already. Ashley, why don't you try the new tech board? I think it's more your size. Josh, you and I can ride those two old long boards I just bought at a yard sale. They're vintage and I'll bet we can hang ten on 'em."

"But we have to clean the shop. We can't leave it like this."

"Why?"

"It's a mess. What will customers think?"

Grizz shook his head. "I don't want to react mindlessly. Sometimes Karma guides you, and you've got to steer away from the negative and put yourself in a place where there's good energy. There's a bad vibe here right now, and I'm sure there's a good vibe out in the ocean."

Josh and Ashley stared at him, brows furrowed.

"Think I'm crazy, right?"

"Not crazy, Grizz." Ashley was starting to smile. "Just from a different generation. You don't always make sense to us—but we love you."

"Come on, let's go." Grizz pulled the *Gone Surfin'* sign from behind the counter.

"The jerk! I can't believe he's out here." Josh stared out at the water, his back stiff, jaw quivering.

"He trashes our store; he breaks in and steals stuff, he tags on the window and—and he can just go out there and play like he doesn't have a care in the world?" Ashley was furious and astonished.

Grizz had actually seen the distant figure topped with red hair before the other two, but he hadn't said anything. He knew his younger companions would catch on soon enough. He shaded his eyes and looked over the expanse of the ocean, then pointed a finger. "There's a shoal beneath the water over that way. See how a second set starts peeling away there? Maybe that's where we should line up today."

Neither commented, but Grizz was pretty sure Ashley and Josh both noticed it was the furthest place in the water from Dirk. They didn't say anything more, just sat down and waxed their boards, splashed water to harden the wax, and paddled out to the spot Grizz had indicated.

The waves were even. Not gnarly like the ocean in Huntington Beach is so much of the year, just three-and-four-foot swells peeling south to north like clockwork. Soon, the three had forgotten their woes at the shop, even forgotten the out-of-control young man who had brought them so much misery. Josh and Grizz did stunts on their big, old boards, balancing on one foot, hanging their toes off the side, skipping around. Ashley carved up and down the crests on the new board, squealing with excitement.

"Hey!"

Josh and Grizz turned toward the sound of Ashley's alarmed voice. They were just in time to see her flying into the air, face contorted. Another surfer had just elbowed her off-balance. Even before Grizz recognized the other surfer, he knew.

Dirk.

Grizz and Josh paddled over to the girl.

"Ash, you okay?"

She pulled herself back onto the board, sputtering, rubbing a red mark on her side. "Yeah, I'm okay."

"C'mon," Josh said. "Let's go tell a lifeguard. They'll pull him out of the water."

But just as they turned to paddle in, whistles pierced the air.

"Red flags are up," Grizz noted.

"Wonder why?" Ashley queried. "There's no riptide today."

"Look at that!" Josh pointed. "*Fins*."

Grizz's heart did a funny little flop: the gray triangles sliced through the water, five of them in uneven formation, darting swiftly to and fro. He knew they weren't dolphins.

Sharks.

Everyone in the water scrambled toward shore.

No, not everyone.

One surfer ignored the whistles and activity around him. Instead, he headed further out into the ocean.

"I hope they get him." Ashley's voice was full of disgust.

"You don't mean that," Josh retorted.

She just glared and paddled toward the beach.

But Grizz stood frozen, his eyes fixed on Dirk. The glistening, darting fins were swerving toward the lone figure. "They're onto him."

"C'mon, Grizz—hurry, get out of the water." Ashley's voice was frantic.

Grizz barely heard her; his eyes fastened toward the tragic drama.

A grey mass flashed out of the green water, knocked the red-headed boy off his board. Grizz turned and paddled furiously toward the attack.

"Grizz!" He heard the voices of Josh and Ashley receding behind him, and in the distance, the sound of an approaching Jet Ski®.

That lifeguard won't make it in time, Grizz thought to himself. *I've never abandoned a surfer in trouble all these years—I'm not gonna' start now. Hope the universe is on our side today.* Grizz scooped water with all his might. Ahead, he saw an arm flailing beside a drifting board; fins and tails of enormous fish darted back and forth around the victim.

A wall of water swooshed toward him; Grizz shoved down on the front of his board, duck-diving through the wave. *Sure hope those sharks don't have friends waiting under here,* he thought as the water poured over his head.

A moment later he popped to the surface. The Jet Ski® sounds drew nearer.

His heart beating, not from exertion but raw fear, Grizz pulled himself into the middle of the roiling water. He saw the boy's body floating, a red stream leaking into the water from a gash on his leg. Grizz reached over to pull Dirk onto his board. He grunted; for a kid his size, Dirk was awful heavy.

An ugly black snout and a row of razor-sharp teeth popped out of the water beside him. Holding the unconscious boy with his left hand, Grizz punched hard as he could with his right. He felt the skin atop his fingers connect with the sand-paper hide of the enormous fish. The huge creature spun in the water, splashed away in the other direction.

With the boy sprawled across his board, Grizz turned toward shore. Five fins circled around him. *Blood*, he thought. *They smell it. God, don't let them attack.*

Gasping for breath, he paddled desperately.

Wham.

A grey mass hurtled against the fiber shell, almost knocking Grizz and his wounded cargo off the board. Grizz breathed the fishy air that rushed against his face in the predator's wake. Struggling for breath, Grizz paddled harder.

From the corner of his eye, he saw a Jet Ski® drawing near. "Grab this rope. Hold on!" a lifeguard yelled.

Grizz grabbed the nylon cord the lifeguard threw and wrapped it around his wrist. With one arm he grasped the sticky waxed rails of his board, with the other he held firmly onto the wounded young man. The guard revved his tiny vessel, and they began moving rapidly toward shore, leaving the lethal pack behind them.

Grizz looked down at Dirk's white face. *Kid's in shock.* He glanced at the gash on the boy's leg, but quickly averted his eyes.

"Hang on, Dirk." He said, leaning down close to the boy's ear. "I don't know if you can hear me, but we're almost ashore. They've got an ambulance waiting. Don't give up now."

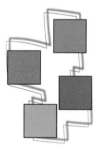

How Is Conduct Disorder Treated?

Treatment of young people with conduct disorder can be complex and challenging. Depending on the severity of the behaviors, treatment can be provided in a variety of settings—home, school, or a residential facility. The young person's uncooperative attitude, fear, and distrust of adults complicates treatment. In developing a comprehensive treatment plan, an adolescent psychiatrist may use information from

Teens with conduct disorder are uncooperative and distrustful of adults. Treatment can therefore be a challenge.

Research shows that most children with conduct disorder grow up to do well as adults.

the adolescent, family, teachers, and other medical specialties to understand the causes of the disorder.

Behavior therapy and **psychotherapy** are usually necessary to help the adolescent appropriately express and control anger. Special education may be needed for young people with learning disabilities. Parents often need expert assistance in devising and carrying out special management and educational programs in the home and at school. Treatment may also include medication in some individuals, especially those who have difficulty paying attention, impulse problems, or depression.

Treatment is rarely quick, since establishing new attitudes and behavior patterns takes time. However, early treatment offers a young person a better chance for considerable improvement and hope for a more successful future.

Conduct Disorder Research

Recent research on conduct disorder has been promising. It has shown that most children and adolescents with conduct disorder do not grow up to have behavioral problems or problems with the law as adults; most of these young people do well as adults, both socially and occupationally.

Researchers are also gaining a better understanding of the causes of conduct disorder, as well as aggressive behavior more generally. Conduct disorder has both genetic and environmental components. Although the disorder is more common among the children of adults who themselves exhibited conduct problems when they were young, researchers believe many other factors contribute to the development of the disorder in addition to heredity. For example, youth with conduct disorder appear to have deficits in processing social information or social cues, and some may have been rejected by peers as young children.

The most successful treatment approaches intervene as early as possible, are structured and intensive, and address the multiple contexts in which young people with this disorder exhibit problem behaviors, including the family, school, and community. Examples of effective treatment approaches include functional family therapy, **multisystemic therapy**, and cognitive behavioral approaches which focus on building skills such as anger management. Pharmacological intervention alone is not sufficient for the treatment of conduct disorder, but medications may have a role

A child whose father had conduct problems in his youth is more likely to exhibit problems himself.

Some adolescents develop conduct disorder as a result of being rejected by peers when younger.

Pharmacological intervention alone is not enough to treat conduct disorder. Rather, effective treatment must include a variety of approaches.

to play in a young person's ability to overcome his disorder.

The Importance of Assessment

Assessment of conduct disorder—or any emotional or behavioral disorder—should be done by a mental health professional, preferably one who is trained in adolescent mental health. The assessment process should include observation of the individual, discussion with the individual and family, the use of **standardized instruments** or structured diagnostic interviews, and history-taking, including a complete

A therapist will work with the teen on cognitive-behavioral approaches such as anger management.

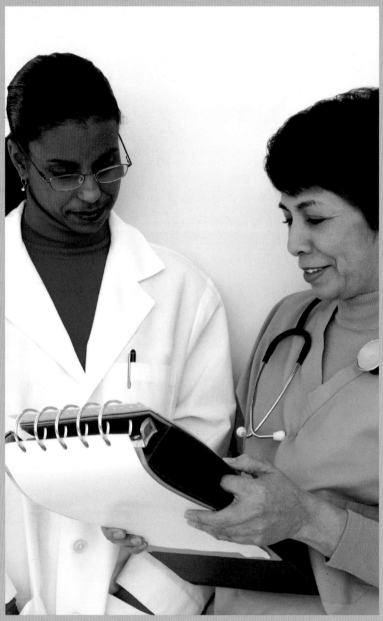

Careful assessment and accurate diagnosis are important first steps in treatment of conduct disorder.

medical and family social history. When assessing and diagnosing any childhood or adolescent emotional or behavioral disorder, the mental health professional considers the social and economic context in which a child's behavior occurs. Cultural expectations and challenges may influence a young person's behavior; behaviors that may be appropriate in some home settings may be completely inappropriate at school or in the larger community.

For young people with conduct disorders, accurate assessment and appropriate, individualized treatment are vital steps in the road to successful adulthood. According to federal law, treatment must be always provided in the least restrictive setting possible. In other words, the school district must make an effort to meet an individual's needs in the regular classroom if at all possible.

Chapter 6
Old Acquaintances

on't tell me what to do. I'm sick of it."

"But the doctor said—"

"Forget the doctor."

"Dirk—"

"And forget you. Get out of here. Now."

Grizz stood outside the hospital room, listening to the angry voices from the other side of the door. There was a moment of silence, and then the door swung open. A tall, thin man practically bowled Grizz over as he hurried out of the room. For an instant, Grizz and the man were face-to-face, just inches away. The man's steel-grey eyes locked with Grizz's. They both stepped back to regain composure.

"Why, Grizz."

"Well, if it isn't Tim Hayden."

"Hey."

"Hey yourself."

"Dude."

"Long time."

Grizz shifted his weight, feeling awkward.

"It's been years."

"Decades."

"I hear you're big in surfing circles."

"Least circles 'round here. What you been up to?"

"Got out of the service. Been selling insurance."

Another long uncomfortable pause.

"How's your son?"

"A lot better than he was ten days ago, when they brought him in." Tim sucked in a breath and scratched at his close-cropped hair. "Grizz—thanks. You saved my son's life out there."

Grizz shrugged. "Soul surfer's way."

"Yeah, yeah. But there's not many men would've done it. Heck of a thing. Right in the middle of a pack of sharks. Took real courage."

"I didn't really think."

Tim shook his head. "You must've been scared witless, least I would have been. But you did it anyway."

Grizz shrugged again and changed the subject. "He sounds pretty upset in there."

"He's always mad at someone—been in trouble with the world since he hit adolescence."

"Not in childhood?"

"No, believe it or not, he was a great kid—until about age fourteen. And then . . . it's like our Dr. Jekyll became Mr. Hyde."

"He really changed, huh?"

"You can't imagine what it was like living with him. He wouldn't follow the rules—any rules. Always mad. He'd fly into rages and break things. One day, he got so furious he slapped his mom." Tim looked down at the ground. "That's when Shelly left us. But she and I hadn't been doing so great for years. I did some pretty dumb things in our marriage too, I guess."

"Hey Tim, you don't have to feel bad around me. Heck, man—I've had three old ladies and none of 'em stuck long enough to have kids. You did better than I have in the marrying game."

Tim flashed a grateful smile. "We might have made it, but. . ." He spoke quietly so sound wouldn't carry through the door. "Dirk made things impossible. It was like he picked up on all our tensions—saw all the weak spots between us and exploited them. Our marriage didn't stand a chance."

"Well," Grizz said, "guess I better get in there and see him."

"Thanks again, dude."

"Least I can do for an old friend."

Their eyes met.

"Hey Grizz . . ."

"Yeah, Tim?"

"Think maybe that was your problem?"

"Maybe. I was wondering myself."

"You turned out all right. I mean, look at you. Successful businessman, famous old-school surfer, everyone in Huntington Beach loves you, man."

"You're totally exaggerating."

"Not. You turned out great . . . better than I have. And that kinda' gives me hope for my son."

"There's always hope, dude."

Tim nodded, headed for the elevator. Grizz pushed the door open and entered.

"Grizz," Dirk greeted him from the bed.

"Well, you're looking better every time I see you."

"I moved my toes today."

"The shark missed a few tendons, huh?"

"They say if I do lots of physical therapy, maybe I'll be able to ride the waves again."

"Awesome."

"Totally."

"And your dad says you've been seeing a counselor here?" Grizz asked as calmly as he could, hoping Dirk wouldn't fly off the handle.

"Oh, yeah."

"She's helpful?"

"She's hot!"

"Hot?"

"Yeah, I mean, for an older chick, you know, she must be like thirty or something."

"Uh, yeah. That's not really why I'm asking."

"She's smokin.' She has these great—"

"*Dirk.*"

"Huh?"

"I'm not interested in the psychologist's looks. I'm wondering if she's helped you talking about . . . uh . . . you know, life, and why you're so angry all the time."

"Oh, yeah. I've got some condition . . . uh . . . conflict disorder or, somethin' like that."

"I think your father said, 'conduct disorder.'"

"Yeah. Right. Whatever. It's pretty cool knowing that."

"It is?"

"Yeah, like there's a reason I'm mad all the time." Grizz thought Dirk's face looked more relaxed than he'd ever seen him before. "My whole life, people been tellin' me I'm bad—cops, teachers, my mom, my old man, chicks' moms, everyone tellin' me what a delinquent I am. This is the first time someone looked at it all deeper, took time to connect the dots."

"So you think you might be able to change all that, turn your life around?"

"Yeah, the doc thinks so."

Grizz flashed a grin. "Well, that would be good news for the rest of us."

"I'm a pain-in-the-you-know-what, aren't I?"

"You can't even imagine. But then, you're not the first or the only one. I was difficult to put up with when I was your age."

Grizz saw Dirk eyes studying his face. "Hey. You know my old man. When he left just now and bumped into you— I saw—you two know each other."

Grizz shrugged.

"You never told me."

"Never asked."

"When did you meet?"

"Oh, I think in sixty-five or sixty-six."

"High school?"

"Yeah."

"You hang together?"

"Yeah. We were pretty tight, once."

"No crap? What was my old man like? Was he a jerk then like he is now?"

"Nope."

"You?"

"Dope smoking, sex-crazed, shoplifting, mad-at-the-world juvenile delinquent."

"Really? If he was cool back then, why'd he hang with you?"

"Maybe he saw potential in me. He was the only kid at Shore View who thought I could be something. Everyone else hated my guts. Even my folks. He's the only one that cared about me back then."

Dirk shook his head. "Sure you have the right person?"

Grizz chuckled, but then he saw the expression on Dirk's face change. "You *knew*—when we met."

"Huh?"

"When I bumped into you on the shore, you saw me and said to yourself, 'That's Tim's kid. I'm gonna' do my old friend a favor and straighten out his son.' Didn't you?" Dirk's voice was outraged.

"Dirk, it's not like—"

But Dirk clearly wasn't listening. He was shouting now. "You never liked me. Just thought of my old man. I'm just your project."

"Dirk, Listen."

"GET OUT NOW!" Dirk threw a punch at Grizz, tearing an IV out of his arm, bringing an attached piece of medical equipment onto the floor with a crash. Grizz easily evaded the weak, hampered punch, but blood spurted from Dirk's arm. An alarm buzzed, and orderlies ran into the room.

Time to leave, Grizz decided. "Seeya, kid!" he shouted on his way out the door.

He could still hear Dirk screaming obscenities at the hospital workers when he was all the way down the long hall.

Well, he's learning some new things. Maybe this hospital stay will help him. All things work for the good, Grizz mused as he headed down the hallway. *Would be nice to meet his counselor—kid's got me curious now.* He took the elevator down to ground level, exited the building, and pulled out a clove cigarette.

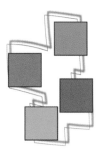

Treating Conduct Disorder with Medication

Although there is no pill a person can take that will make conduct disorder simply go away, a few drugs are used that may help an individual to more effectively participate in behavioral treatment programs. These drugs are lithium, methylphenidate, carbamazepine, and clonidine. All of these drugs have side effects but they are safe when used appropriately.

A child and her parents may be relieved to hear a diagnosis of conduct disorder, because it offers an explanation and hope for a solution to their problems.

Since most young people with conduct disorders also have some other psychiatric disorder (called a "comorbid disorder"), treating these comorbid disorders effectively is an essential step in treatment.

Conduct Disorder with ADHD

Young people who have both conduct disorder and ADHD have been successfully treated with stimulants. Although this type of medical intervention does not remove all symptoms, it can make a big difference. It often means that the nonmedical interventions will work much better.

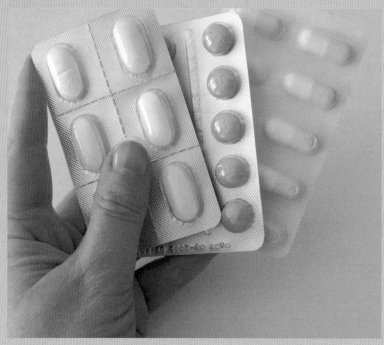

There is no pill that can make conduct disorder disappear.

Many youth with conduct disorder also struggle with substance abuse. Treating the substance abuse as well will be an important part of treatment.

A young person with conduct disorder who is also depressed will have better luck with treatment if she first receives antidepressants.

Conduct Disorder with Depression

Recent studies have shown that when young people have both conduct disorders and depression, they can address the behaviors that spring from their conduct disorder if they receive antidepressants. These medications, of which Prozac® is probably the best known, help change the chemical balances in the brain, stabilizing emotions. Since depression can make it difficult for a person to function, a person whose depression has been treated will be better able to work on the behavioral issues caused by a conduct disorder.

Chapter 7
Close Encounter of the Rude Kind

Grizz, you are absolutely, without a doubt, the craziest dude in Surf City."

Grizz smiled at Josh's remark and busied himself arranging videos under the counter.

"I mean it. We've got a lotta wacked-out street people and smack-heads and gonzo surfer types but no one—and I mean no one—is crazy like you."

Grizz grinned; he took Josh's words as a compliment.

"He trashes the place, tags the windows, steals, cusses you out after you save his life, and you let Dirk work here again." Josh shook his head so hard his ponytail whipped back and forth. "It's nuts."

"Thought you were one of those born-again Christians, Josh."

"I am. Go to Calvary Vineyard Church."

"Didn't Jesus say something about 'love your enemies'?"

"Yeah. . . ." Josh looked embarrassed. "Sorry."

The front door swung open, chimes signaling its motion. Dirk limped in, a cigarette wafting smoke from his hand.

"Put the cig out," Grizz told him. "Too much flammable stuff in this shop. That's why I smoke outside. Same goes for you."

Dirk dropped the smoking object onto the floor and ground it with his sandal. Josh winced, no doubt thinking of how he had just mopped. "Hey," Dirk said, "be glad it isn't ganja." He turned to Grizz. "We got boards to work on?"

"Yeah, I've got three new big ones all shaped and glassed. Just gotta' mount the skegs on 'em. You wanta do that?"

"Sure. Hey, you seen the new ones from Maui Style? Big old-school fins with a real sharp cut-back at the top?"

"I've got a pack of 'em under the sawhorses in the back room. Think we should go with those?"

Dirk nodded. The kid's learning the trade alright, Grizz thought.

Josh was staring out the window; the other two followed his gaze. A van pulled up in front of the store: classic surf bus, shiny and fancy.

"Wow," Josh exclaimed, "that musta cost a fortune. They're getting harder and harder to find in good shape." Josh's old van was a rolling rust bucket.

Two guys got out of the van, clad in expensive clothes and sun glasses. "It's Bret Stender driving that beauty, and Cain Williams is with him," Josh announced.

"Rich jerks," Dirk added under his breath.

"They can be mean," Josh acknowledged.

The door chimed as they entered the store. "Hey, you got a copy of that new Wave Jams CD?" asked Bret, the shorter boy.

"Yeah, just came in the mail this morning." Grizz bent down behind the counter to look for it.

Cain turned toward Dirk, an insolent smirk on his face. "Well . . . it's Dirk the Jerk. Or should we call you Gimpy? What are you doing here?"

Dirk stiffened, took a deep breath, eyes bulging almost out of their sockets.

Cain leered at him. "Wanna take me on, don't you? Go ahead. Take a swing at me—I'll kickya right in the hole that shark took out."

Dirk was hyperventilating. Josh stepped in front of him. "Steady, dude—it's not worth it."

Grizz overheard, and straightened up from behind the counter. "I think it's time for you guys to leave."

"Hey, what about my CD?" asked Bret.

"You're insulting my employee. I'm asking you to leave my store," Grizz replied in a level voice.

"You're letting this loser work in your store?"

"Nope. Kickin' one out. Hit the road." Grizz's voice was firm.

The two strode toward the exit, and then, before the door swung shut, Cain started dragging his leg in an exaggerated pantomime of Dirk's limp. The two pointed at the red-headed boy and laughed. They both walked away around the corner, Cain still mocking Dirk's affliction.

Dirk's face was red as his hair.

"Ignore them," Grizz said.

Dirk limped quickly into the back of the shop. Grizz and Josh stared at one another, worried. An instant later, Dirk hobbled back into the front of the store, clutching an aluminum baseball bat that Grizz used to flatten new boards. Dirk cast a smoldering glance at the glistening vehicle still parked in front of the store. It was one of those old classic vans with glass panels all around, and a second row of little windows on the top to let light in: a small fortune in rare, hard-to-repair auto glass.

"Whoa. Dude, don't," Josh begged.

Dirk strode to the door, flung it open.

"Dirk." Grizz's voice stopped the boy mid-step. "I trust you, kid. You can do the right thing now."

The sky was still blue and air warm as Grizz put his well-worn brass key in the knob to lock up Grizzly Surf Shop for the night. It was a slow day, so he had sent Dirk home earlier in the afternoon. Grizz sniffed at the sea breeze and decided to walk home along the sidewalk fronting the beaches. It wasn't the direct way, but no one was waiting for him at home except Gidget and Moonie, his nappy-haired dogs.

He passed by a concrete bench, then paused. A thin man with short hair and grey eyes sat looking out to sea. Grizz eased down next to him.

"Hey, Tim."

"Hiya there, Grizz."

"Cigarette?" Grizz pulled a crumpled pack from the pocket of his Hawaiian shirt.

"No way. Those'll kill you."

"Yep." Grizz pulled a lighter from his shorts and lit up. "So how ya doing?"

"Life's okay. You?"

"Never been better."

The two men sat quietly for several minutes, soaking in the beauty of the sunny afternoon.

"So," Grizz spoke up, "Dirk tells me he's moved back in with you. Is that going okay?"

Tim shrugged. "It's never relaxing living with Dirk—but it is smoother than before. Last night he threw a fit because

I wanted to watch sports on the big screen and he had a new video game he wanted to play on it. He threw the television remote in the hot tub."

"What did you do then?"

"Told him he couldn't use the big screen for a week."

"And then?"

"He cussed at me and walked out of the house. He came back sober, though—I give him credit for that. And he apologized this morning and said he'd buy a new remote for us."

"That does sound like progress. Guess the hospital folks are making a difference, huh?"

"They really are. He's taking a drug now, Risperidal. I worry about the side effects, but I think that's helping. They're also helping him fight his addictions."

Grizz chuckled. "Yeah, he brought a little bag of pills with him to the store on Tuesday. I thought for sure he was taking acid or something. But he explained, so we're cool. Is he still seeing the psychologist?"

"Yeah, he can hardly wait for his weekly visits. He's got all kinds of crazy thoughts about her, but at least he's getting treatment. And he does listen. How is he doing at your shop?"

"He's making progress. He almost took a bat to a customer's van, but then he got control at the last moment, so nothing happened. And the kid's a whiz at shaping. Actually, I'm thinking I should let him make boards and I'll sell them. That would make us both happier, I think."

Tim shaded his eyes and looked at the beach in front of them. "There's Dirk now—with his board. He told me the physical therapist gave him the green light to get back in the water. But who's the young woman with him?"

"Oh, that's Keisha Arellano."

"The teen girl's champion?"

"The same."

"I didn't know my son was friends with her."

"Actually, she hated his guts not long ago. He made some crude remarks. But after the shark attack, she came into the shop to ask about him. He was limping around the store and a lot more humble. She offered to help him get going in the waves again. I think it's female nurturing instinct or something. Anyway, I'm hoping they'll hit it off so I can steal her back from Wavetech."

"My son does have a way with the women. Amazing, given how he antagonizes everyone. And look at us—two old guys, alone on a bench."

Grizz smiled. "I don't know about you, but I'm always looking for the next Mrs. Sanchez. It's just hard to find women with good taste."

They both chuckled, then sat in a companionable silence. They watched the young man limp into the water, the girl beside with her hand on his back, steadying him. Then the two teens lay on their boards, paddled through a set of small waves, and Grizz lost sight of them in the blazing reflection of the sun setting toward the water.

Hope there's no sharks out there, the soul surfer reflected, but the kid's got good Karma. He's gonna do okay.

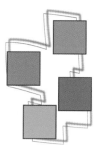

Drugs That Counteract Violence

There are some drugs that have been tested in adults and children who are violent and aggressive for a variety of reasons, whether because of brain damage, a personality disorder, or conduct disorder. These drugs are only used when nothing else works.

Atypical Antipsychotics

These drugs were first used for schizophrenia, and that is how they got this name. They are now commonly

Adolescents who are extremely violent and aggressive may be prescribed antipsychotic drugs.

Weight gain is one of the most common side effects when teens begin taking atypical antipsychotics.

used for many conditions where people are not psychotic. All of them can have serious side effects. As a result, they are not used for small problems.

- risperidone (Risperidal)
- olanzapine (Zyprexa)
- quetiapine (Seroquel)

Side Effects of the Atypical Antipsychotics

Weight gain is the biggest problem when young people take these drug. Not all kids gain weight, but a fair number may put on thirty pounds or more. Since obesity can have serious health consequences, this side effect cannot be dismissed; what's more,

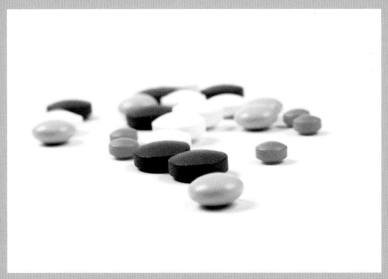

All of the atypical antipsychotics pose the risk of serious side effects.

adolescents who are particularly sensitive about their physical appearance may suffer loss of self-esteem as a result of weight gain.

Stiffness, restlessness, and tremors can also be caused by these drugs. They can also cause a sudden stiffening of the body, a terrifying condition that is reversible if the dosage is reduced or the drug is stopped.

Elevated cholesterol and triglycerides can occur, even when the individual does not gain weight. Zyprexa is the most likely to cause this, followed by Seroquel, and the least likely is Risperidal. Again, elevated cholesterol can have serious health consequences.

Diabetes is another serious complication that can be brought on by these medications. Zyprexa is the most likely to cause this, followed by Seroquel, and least likely is Risperidal. In the large study of Risperidal, not one child out of over 500 developed diabetes.

Tardive dyskinesia is a movement disorder where people can have chewing movements of the mouth, grimacing, head movements, trunk movements, and hand movements. The movements are not jerky but smooth and rhythmic. Risperidal is the most likely to cause this, while the other two are very unlikely to cause it. In the large study of Risperidal, not one child out of over 500 developed this problem.

Older Mood Stabilizers

Drugs like lithium may be prescribed when the atypical antipsychotics don't work or are not tolerated. Lithium can prevent suicide, and counteract depression and

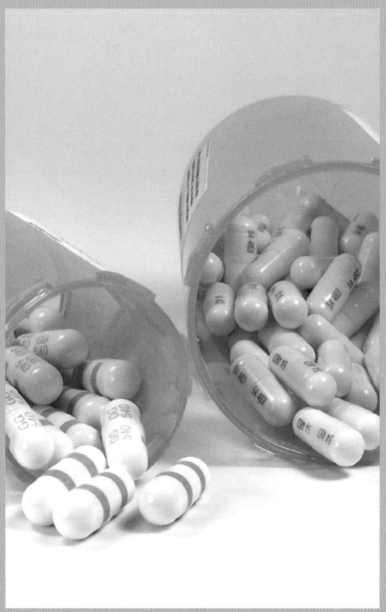

Lithium might be prescribed if atypical antipsychotics are not effective. Again, lithium has numerous possible side effects.

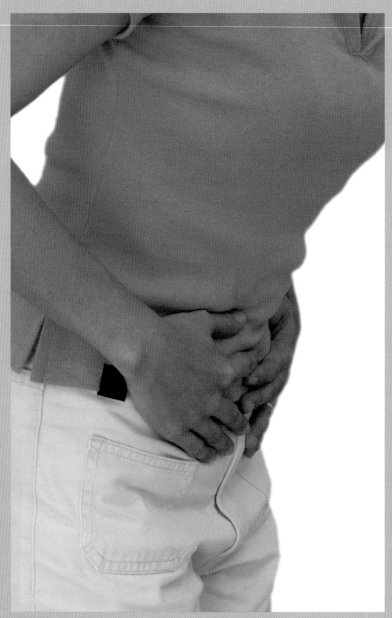

Nausea, vomiting and diarrhea are common side effects of
lithium.

mania, but it has numerous side effects. Some of these are merely a nuisance—like nausea, vomiting, diarrhea, shakiness, and balance problems. It can also cause weight gain and bedwetting, and it can cause or worsen acne and **psoriasis**. Even worse, though, lithium can damage the kidneys. At high levels, the drug can affect the brain, making people experience confusion, slow thinking, and poor balance.

None of the mood stabilizers are as safe as doctors would like. When weighing the risks of the medication, doctors, families, and adolescents need to balance the risk of the untreated condition versus the risk of the medication. In severe cases, the risk of the disorder far exceeds the risk of the medication. In very mild cases, it is best to try to get by without these drugs.

When mood stabilizers don't work, though, even when added to atypical antipsychotics, other drugs may be tried.

Clonidine

This drug was originally developed for treating blood pressure; it is very safe, and it turns out to be useful for a lot of things, including **tics**, severe ADHD, detoxifying heroin addicts, menopausal symptoms, and sometimes autism with hyperactivity or severe aggression.

Unfortunately, about one out of every ten to twenty people who take this drug will become depressed. For this reason, young people who are taking this drug must be carefully monitored. Young

A diagnosis of conduct disorder is not the end of the world for a teen. In fact, with proper treatment and support, she will likely grow up to be a successful and happy adult.

people taking Clonidine should also have their blood pressure and pulse rate checked regularly, since the medication can lower the pulse and blood pressure.

If all these drugs have side effects, why use them?

They shouldn't be used if a young person can learn to overcome his conduct disorder with the help of counseling and behavioral interventions. But if these alone aren't working, then drugs may give the young person the help he needs to make important changes in his life.

Conduct disorder is a serious condition. It can also be a dangerous one, because of the risks it brings to the individual's life. However, there is hope. People with this disorder can grow up to be functioning adults with much to offer the world.

Glossary

ADHD: Attention deficit/hyperactivity disorder, a developmental and behavioral disorder, characterized by poor concentration, distractibility, hyperactivity, and impulsiveness.

behavior therapy: Therapy that focuses on the treatment of observable behaviors instead of the underlying psychological processes and aims to substitute desirable responses for undesirable ones.

bipolar disorder: A disorder characterized by periods of mania—extreme, giddy happiness—alternating with periods of depression.

cognitive-behavioral therapy: A form of therapy in which the goal is to decrease symptoms by correcting distorted thinking based on negative self-image and expectations.

mania: Excessive excitement or enthusiasm.

multisystemic therapy: A family- and community-based treatment that addresses the multiple causes of serious antisocial behavior and addresses problems as they occur in each area, or system, of the individual's life.

norms: Standards, models or patterns regarded by society as normal.

post-traumatic stress disorder: A psychological disorder affecting individuals who have experienced or witnessed profoundly traumatic events, characterized by recurrent flashbacks of the traumatic event, nightmares, irritability, anxiety, fatigue, forgetfulness, and social withdrawal.

psoriasis: A common, chronic skin disease characterized by scaly patches.

psychotherapy: The treatment of psychological disorders through talking, as psychoanalysis, group therapy, or behavioral therapy.

respite: To relieve momentarily, especially from anything distressing or troublesome.

standardized instruments: Tools or tests that are used in the same way by every researcher and measure the same figures (ie height, effectiveness of therapy), so that data from two different experiments may be compared accurately.

tics: Habitual, uncontrollable, muscular movements, usually of the face, arms, or legs.

Tourette's syndrome: A neurological disorder characterized by recurrent involuntary movements, including multiple neck jerks and sometimes vocal tics, as grunts, barks, or words.

Further Reading

Berstein, Jeffrey. *10 days to a Less Defiant Child.* New York: Marlowe & Company, 2006.

Greene, Ross W. *The Explosive Child: A New Approach for Understanding and Parenting Easily Frustrated, Chronically Inflexible Children.* New York: Harper, 2001.

Greene, Ross W. and J. Stuart Ablon. *Treating Explosive Kids: The Collaborative Problem-Solving Approach.* New York: The Guilford Press, 2006.

Hagener, Nancy A. *The Dance of Defiance: A Mother and Son Journey with Oppositional Defiant Disorder.* St. Pete Beach, Fla.: Shamrock, 2005.

O'Reilly, Dermot, and Brian Sheldon. *Conduct Disorder And Behavioural Parent Training: Research And Practice.* London, UK and Philadelphia, PA: Jessica Kingsley Publishers, 2005.

Riley, Douglas. *The Defiant Child: A Parent's Guide to Oppositional Defiant Disorder.* Texas: Taylor Publishing, 1997.

Wells, Ruth Herman. *All the Best Answers for the Worst Kid Problems: Anti Social Youth and Conduct Disorders.* Woodburn, OR: Youth Change, 2003.

For More Information

Conduct Disorders
http://www.conductdisorders.com

Facts for Families
aacap.org/page.ww?section=Facts+for+Families&name=
Facts+for+Families

Kids Mental Health
http://www.kidsmentalhealth.org/
ConductDisorderOppositionalDefiantDisorder.html

National Mental Health Association
www.nmha.org/infoctr/index.cfm

NYU Child Study Center
http://www.aboutourkids.org/aboutour/articles/
about_conduct.html

SAMHSA's National Mental Health Information Center
http://mentalhealth.samhsa.gov/publications/allpubs/
CA-0010/default.asp

Publisher's note:
The Web sites listed on this page were active at the time of publication. The publisher is not responsible for Web sites that have changed their addresses or discontinued operation since the date of publication. The publisher will review and update the Web-site list upon each reprint.

Bibliography

American Academy of Child & Adolescent Psychiatry. "Facts for Families. Conduct Disorder." July 2004. http://aacap.org/page.ww?section=Facts+for+Families&name=Conduct+Disorder

Eddy, J. Mark. *Conduct Disorders: The Latest Assessment and Treatment Strategies.* New York: Compact Clinicals, 2006.

Hill, Jonathan and Barbara Maughan. *Conduct Disorders in Childhood and Adolescence.* New York: Cambridge University Press, 2000.

Lahey, Benjamin. *Causes of Conduct Disorder and Juvenile Delinquency.* New York: Guilford, 2003.

Mental Health: A Report of the Surgeon General. "Disruptive Disorders." http://www.surgeongeneral.gov/library/mentalhealth/chapter3/sec6.html#disruptive

Index

Picture Credits

Artville
        Smallish, Craig: p. 83
fotolia.com
                ctacik: p. 19
                Elisseeva, Elena: p. 97
                Frenk_DanielleKaufmann: p. 100
Gevaert, Eric; p. 38
Jeanblanc, Veronique: p. 98
Letzel, Andre: p. 80
Mucibabic, Vladimir: p. 34
Niezabitowski, Jakub: p. 66
Novakovic, Darko: p. 20
Oates, Lou: p. 82
Raeder, Petra: p. 53
Redel, Stefan: p. 37
Schulz, Jay: p. 49
Thompson, Leah-Anne: p. 65
istock.com
                Darinburt: p. 21
                De Suza, Brendon: p. 81
                Foster, Paige: p. 115
                Ince, Levent: p. 113
                Louie, Nancy: p. 84
                Medina, Lorelyn: p. 116
                Schlax, Nick: p. 22
                Schmidt, Chris: p. 111
Jupiter Images: pp. 54, 63, 64, 77, 78, 99, 112, 118

Authors

Kenneth McIntosh is a freelance writer living in northern Arizona with his family. He has written two dozen educational books, and taught at junior high, high school, and community college levels.

Phyllis Livingston has her master's degree in special education. She has worked with a wide variety of teenagers with various psychiatric disorders, including depression and anxiety.

Series Consultants

Dr. Bridgemohan is an Assistant Professor in Pediatrics at Harvard Medical School and is a Board Certified Developmental-Behavioral Pediatrician on staff in the Developmental Medicine Center at Children's Hospital, Boston. She specializes in assessment and treatment of autism and developmental disorders in young children. Her clinical practice includes children and youth with autism, developmental language disorders, global delays, mental retardation, attentional and learning disorders, anxiety, and depression. Dr. Bridgemohan is Co-director of residency training in Child Development at Children's Hospital, Boston, and is co-editor of "Bright Futures Case Studies for Primary Care Clinicians: Child Development and Behavior," a curriculum used nationwide in Pediatric Residency training programs. Dr. Bridgemohan has also published research and review articles on resident education, toilet training, autism screening, and medical evaluation of children with developmental disorders.

Cindy Croft, M.A.Ed., is the Director of the Center for Inclusive Child Care (CICC) at Concordia University, St. Paul, MN. The CICC is a comprehensive resource network for promoting and supporting inclusive early childhood and school-age programs and providers with Project EXCEPTIONAL training and consultation, and other resources at www.inclusivechildcare. org. In addition to working with the CICC, Ms. Croft is on the faculty at Concordia University and Minneapolis Community and Technical College.